MINDFULNESS

FOR CATS

summersdale

SAM HART

MINDFULNESS FOR CATS

Copyright © Summersdale Publishers Ltd, 2015

With research by Fleur Thompson

Summersdale Publishers Ltd
46 West Street
Chichester
West Sussex
PO19 1RP
UK

www.summersdale.com

Printed and bound in China

ISBN: 978-1-84953-780-3

Substantial discounts on bulk quantities of Summersdale books are available to corporations, professional associations and other organisations. For details contact general enquiries: telephone: +44 (0) 1243 771107, fax: +44 (0) 1243 786300 or email: enquiries@summersdale.com.

To...

From...

TAKE A COUPLE OF MINUTES TO NOTICE YOUR BREATHING. SENSE THE FLOW OF THE BREATH, THE RISE AND FALL OF YOUR BELLY.

RECOGNISE THAT THOUGHTS ARE
SIMPLY THOUGHTS; YOU DON'T NEED TO
BELIEVE THEM OR REACT TO THEM.

IF YOU ARE FEELING ANXIOUS,
TAKE A FEW BREATHS AND ON EVERY
OUT-BREATH SAY, 'I AM AT PEACE.'

AS YOU GO ABOUT YOUR DAY, SEND SILENT MESSAGES OF LOVE TO THOSE AROUND YOU — WHETHER THEY ARE STRANGERS OR FRIENDS.

ACCEPT YOURSELF AS YOU ARE,
AND YOU WILL FIND PEACE.

EVERYTHING YOU DO
CAN BE DONE BETTER FROM
A PLACE OF RELAXATION.

WHEN YOU FEEL LIKE HIDING FROM THE WORLD, FIND A QUIET PLACE AND SIMPLY BE.

LOOKING AT THE BEAUTY OF THE
WORLD AROUND YOU IS THE FIRST
STEP TO BECOMING MINDFUL.

IT IS POSSIBLE TO LIVE HAPPILY EVER AFTER ON A DAY-TO-DAY BASIS.

BE HAPPY IN THE MOMENT,
THAT'S ENOUGH. EACH MOMENT
IS ALL WE NEED, NO MORE.

IF YOU'RE HAVING A BUSY DAY, TAKE A FEW MINUTES TO RELAX YOUR FACIAL MUSCLES AND JUST FOCUS ON YOUR BREATHING.

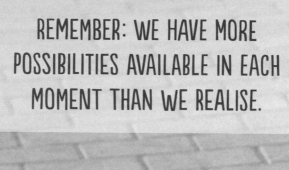

REMEMBER: WE HAVE MORE POSSIBILITIES AVAILABLE IN EACH MOMENT THAN WE REALISE.

CULTIVATE YOUR FRIENDSHIPS AND
THEY WILL BLOSSOM.

STOP TO ADMIRE THE VIEW THAT YOU SEE EVERY DAY — SEE HOW MANY NEW THINGS YOU NOTICE.

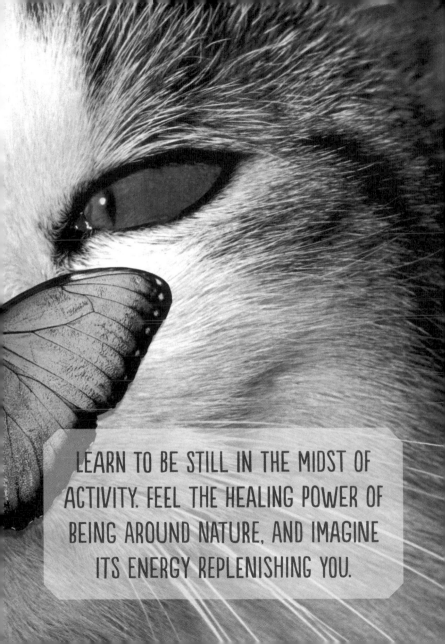

LEARN TO BE STILL IN THE MIDST OF ACTIVITY. FEEL THE HEALING POWER OF BEING AROUND NATURE, AND IMAGINE ITS ENERGY REPLENISHING YOU.

HELP OTHERS TO REALISE THAT IF THEY
ARE PREOCCUPIED WITH SOMETHING,
THEY CANNOT ENJOY THE WORLD.

ALWAYS BE CURIOUS AND INTERESTED
IN THE PEOPLE YOU MEET — TAKE TIME
GETTING TO KNOW LIKE MINDS.

IMAGINE YOURSELF SOARING
LIKE A BIRD — FEEL THE
FREEDOM THIS BRINGS.

DO LESS — DO IT MORE
SLOWLY, MORE FULLY AND
WITH MORE CONCENTRATION.

GET OUT OF YOUR HEAD
AND INTO YOUR HEART.
THINK LESS AND FEEL MORE.

TAKE SOME TIME TO SIMPLY BE.

IMAGINE THAT WITHIN YOUR HEART YOU CARRY AROUND A LIGHTED CANDLE. SEE OTHERS TOO, WITH THEIR FLAMES AGLOW. APPRECIATE THE LIGHT IN EVERYONE!

LAUGH AT YOURSELF WHEN YOU DISCOVER HOW MUCH NEGATIVITY YOU CARRY IN YOUR MIND.

ENJOY BEING NEAR WATER.
LISTEN TO THE SOUND OF IT
FLOWING AND LAPPING.

WHEN YOUR MIND STARTS TO
FLAG, HAVE A GOOD STRETCH.

MAKE ROOM FOR FUN —
IT'S AN IMPORTANT PART OF
LIVING A BALANCED LIFE.

FIND A FAVOURITE PLACE TO SIT
AND BE CALM. ALLOW YOURSELF
TO SPEND A FEW MINUTES THERE
AS OFTEN AS YOU CAN.

MAKE TODAY A 'NO RUSH' DAY. HANDLE EACH OF YOUR ACTIVITIES WITH THE ATTENTION AND CARE THEY DESERVE.

BE PRESENT — FIND ETERNITY
IN EVERY MOMENT.

TAKE PLEASURE IN THE SIMPLE THINGS AROUND YOU. SEEK TO EXPAND YOUR HEART AND MIND, NOT YOUR POSSESSIONS.

WHEN EXTERNAL DISTRACTIONS
THREATEN TO THROW YOU OFF
BALANCE, CHOOSE TO BE STILL AND
CONNECT TO YOUR INNER PEACE.

BE ESPECIALLY AWARE OF YOUR JUDGEMENTS AND EXPECTATIONS TODAY. LET GO OF THE STRESS OF PERFECTIONISM.

WHEN OUR MINDS ARE ENGULFED WITH
STORIES OF OUR PAST OR FUTURE,
WE ARE MISSING THE EXPERIENCE
OF THE MOMENT. KEEP REMEMBERING
THE MOMENTS YOU ARE IN.

FOCUS ON AN OBJECT FROM NATURE.
ADMIRE THE WAY IT MOVES AND
MARVEL IN EVERY DETAIL.

LOOK AT EVERYTHING WITH A SENSE OF WONDER AND SURPRISE, LIKE A CHILD SEEING IT FOR THE FIRST TIME.

CELEBRATE TODAY'S SUCCESSES AND ACHIEVEMENTS. ENCOURAGE AND PRAISE YOURSELF BEFORE DASHING ON TO NEW CHALLENGES.

ALLOW YOURSELF SOME TIME
TO PLAY AND HAVE FUN BEFORE
STARTING A BUSY DAY.

IF YOU WANT TO CONQUER THE ANXIETY OF LIFE, LIVE IN THE MOMENT, LIVE IN THE BREATH.

WHEN YOU REALISE THAT
NOTHING IS LACKING, THE WHOLE
WORLD BELONGS TO YOU.

SEEK ADVENTURES THAT OPEN
YOUR HEART AND SOUL, AND
MAKE YOU FEEL ALIVE.

THERE IS JOY IN JUST BEING.

SEEK OUT OBJECTS THAT ATTRACT YOU IN NATURE. BRING INTO SHARP FOCUS YOUR SENSES OF SIGHT, SOUND, SMELL, TOUCH AND TASTE.

HAVE A MIND THAT IS OPEN TO
EVERYTHING, AND ATTACHED TO NOTHING.

SPREAD GOODWILL AND HAPPINESS BY PERFORMING SMALL ACTS OF KINDNESS, SUCH AS OPENING A DOOR OR GIVING SOMEONE A BIG SMILE.

If you're interested in finding out more
about our books, find us on Facebook
at **Summersdale Publishers** and follow
us on Twitter at **@Summersdale**.

www.summersdale.com